PIANO · VOCAL · GUITAR

White Christmas

MOVIE VOCAL SELECTIONS

ISBN 978-0-634-02568-6

PARAMOUNT PRESENTS IRVING BERLIN'S "WHITE CHRISTMAS"
Starring BING CROSBY DANNY KAYE ROSEMARY CLOONEY VERA-ELLEN with DEAN JAGGER
Lyrics and Music by IRVING BERLIN Produced by ROBERT EMMETT DOLAN
Directed by MICHAEL CURTIZ Dances and Musical Numbers Staged by ROBERT ALTON
Written for the screen by NORMAN KRASNA, NORMAN PANAMA and MELVIN FRANK
© 1954, Renewed 1982 Paramount Pictures. All Rights Reserved

Irving Berlin Music Company®
www.irvingberlin.com

EXCLUSIVELY DISTRIBUTED BY

7777 W. BLUEMOUND RD. P.O. BOX 13819 MILWAUKEE, WI 53213

Visit Hal Leonard Online at
www.halleonard.com

CONTENTS

The Best Things Happen While You're Dancing
7

Blue Skies
10

Choreography
18

Count Your Blessings Instead of Sheep
15

Gee, I Wish I Was Back in the Army
22

Heat Wave
26

Love, You Didn't Do Right by Me
32

Mandy
38

The Old Man
35

Sisters
42

Snow
50

White Christmas
46

White Christmas

THE HISTORY

The roots of the holiday classic film *White Christmas* go back to the 1933 Broadway revue *As Thousands Cheer*. Irving Berlin collaborated with writer Moss Hart on a plotless succession of scenes based on newspaper stories. One of the show's standout numbers was "Easter Parade," which stylishly depicted the Fifth Avenue fashion ritual as portrayed in a turn-of-the-century rotagravure newspaper section. From that song grew a theatrical revue concept based entirely on holidays, but Berlin and Hart never got the project off the ground.

By the end of the 1930s Irving Berlin had written several Hollywood musicals, including three films for the legendary team of Fred Astaire and Ginger Rogers: *Carefree*, *Top Hat* and *Follow the Fleet*. Berlin, once king of Tin Pan Alley, had become the most powerful songwriter in Hollywood. He remembered that old concept of a musical based on holidays, and pitched it to producer-director Mark Sandrich, by then at Paramount, who previously had directed five of the RKO Astaire-Rogers pictures. Berlin and Sandrich developed the idea as a vehicle for Bing Crosby, with the brilliant twist to team him up with Fred Astaire. The result was the 1942 release *Holiday Inn*, in which Crosby retires from his song-and-dance act to a farm in Connecticut, but gets restless and decides to turn it into a cabaret style nightclub/theatre open only on holidays, with themed revues.

There was a Christmas scene, of course. Berlin reportedly struggled with a song idea for this scene and intently waited for Crosby's opinion of the result. The songwriter needn't have worried. The song, "White Christmas," was the biggest hit in the entire history of 20th century popular music, selling more than any other song for the next 50 years, with over 500 recorded versions in 25 languages.

"White Christmas" was first heard on a 1941 Christmas Day radio broadcast. Though the film wouldn't be released until the summer of 1942, Crosby was more than glad to have the brand new Berlin song on his radio show as a special holiday gift to America. Pearl Harbor had been attacked just three weeks earlier, and the U.S. was overwhelmed with dark concern as the war began in earnest. No copy of the premiere radio broadcast performance survives.

Crosby recorded the song (without the verse) in the studio in May of 1942 with the John Trotter Orchestra. The single was released October 1, 1942, and by October 31 had hit Number 1, where it remained for 11 weeks. A hit Christmas song on Halloween! "White Christmas" was one of the most powerfully emotional songs of separation and longing of wartime America. For millions of people torn apart and sick with worry, the song perfectly summed up the universal longing for peace, family and home. The record was duplicated so many times that the original 1942 master was completely worn out. As a result, in 1947 Crosby re-recorded the song, attempting to carefully duplicate everything about the famous first recording.

Holiday Inn was a hit movie, followed up in 1946 by *Blue Skies*, another Crosby and Astaire film with a Berlin score. A few years later, the Crosby-Astaire-Berlin movie musical formula was launched again. Unfortunately, Fred Astaire had to withdraw due to illness, replaced by Donald O'Connor. Early in production, O'Connor then became ill, and ultimately Danny Kaye stepped in to star with Bing Crosby, Rosemary Clooney and Vera-Ellen. Eight new Berlin songs were filmed, as well as several Berlin chestnuts. The picture, of course, was *White Christmas*, directed by Michael Curtiz. Besides a few musicals, Curtiz directed many dramas in Hollywood, including the Bogart-Bergman classic *Casablanca*.

White Christmas was released in VistaVision, a wide-screen technology of the time. It was an enormous success. The film was the top-grossing release for 1954, and ranked fifth in box-office receipts for the entire decade of the 1950s.

THE PLOT

Bob Wallace (Bing Crosby) and Phil Davis (Danny Kaye) put together a song-and-dance act to boost the morale of their fellow soldiers on Christmas Eve, 1944. Private Davis saves Captain Wallace's life in serious shellfire. Wallace, now in Davis' debt, agrees to keep the act together in civilian life. The two find success on Broadway, and ten years later have a very popular television show.

Bob and Phil are performing in Florida when they fall under the charm of the Haynes sisters, Betty (Rosemary Clooney) and Judy (Vera-Ellen), who trick the two TV celebrities into seeing their act. The sisters travel to perform at an inn in Vermont as Christmas approaches. Phil tricks Bob and everyone else by coming up with a "booking" for the very same inn at the same time as the sisters.... what a coincidence!

It's unseasonably balmy in New England. Since there is no snow, there are no guests at the inn, the show is cancelled, and the sisters are out of a needed job. Just by complete Hollywood chance, the inn is owned by none other than retired General Waverly, the same general Bob and Phil served under during the war. The general is losing so much business he may have to close the inn, and he's quite despondent in his retirement. Bob and Phil still feel enormous loyalty to the older man, and make an appeal on national television to all the men who served under General Waverly to come to his Vermont inn on Christmas Eve. It works. Snow falls.

There's a little bit of romantic intrigue in the coupling up of Betty and Bob, and Phil and Judy, but nothing a Hollywood ending can't iron out. And incidentally, there are several great Irving Berlin numbers along the way...

—Hank Powell

White Christmas

The Best Things Happen
While You're Dancing

Words and Music by
IRVING BERLIN

danc - ing _____ soon be-comes ro - manc - ing _____

_____ when you hold a girl in your arms that

you've nev - er held be - fore. _____

E - ven guys with two left feet _____ come

out al-right if the girl is sweet, __ if by chance their

cheeks should meet __ while danc - ing, _____ prov-ing that the

best things hap - pen while __ you dance. _____

The dance. _____

Blue Skies

Words and Music by
IRVING BERLIN

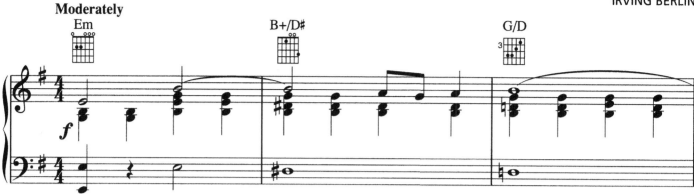

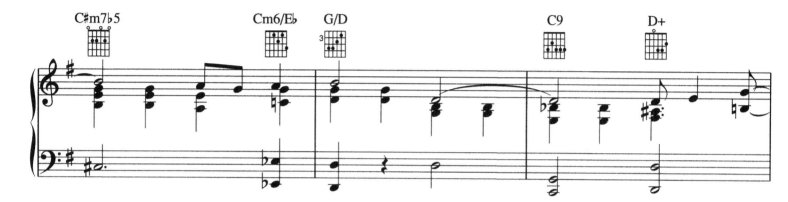

I
I was blue just as blue as I could
I should care just if as the wind blows east or

Count Your Blessings Instead of Sheep

Words and Music by
IRVING BERLIN

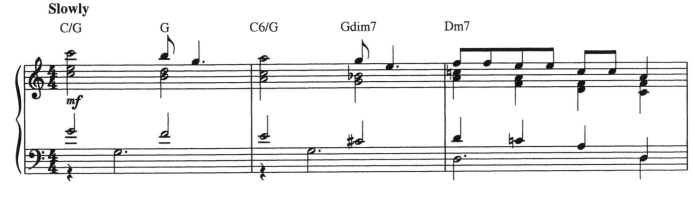

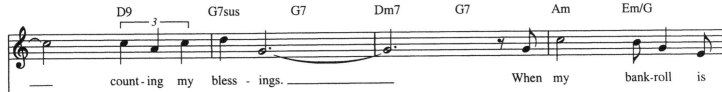

get - ting small, __ I think of when I had none at all. __ And

I fall a - sleep __ count - ing my bless -

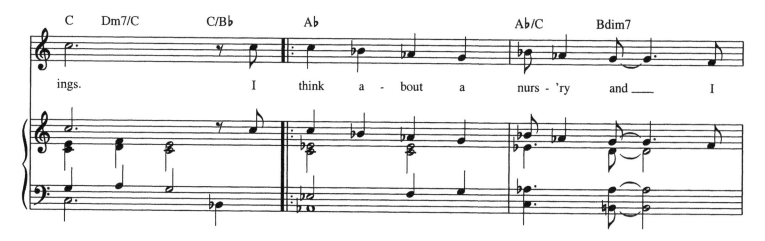

ings. I think a - bout a nurs - 'ry and __ I

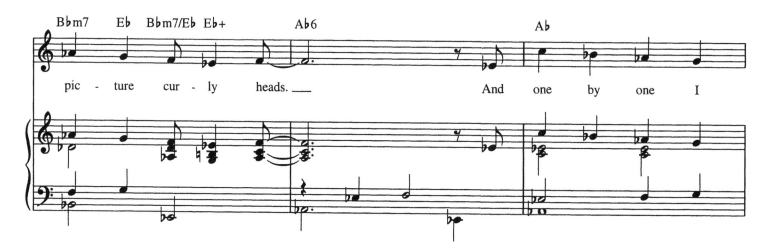

pic - ture cur - ly heads. __ And one by one I

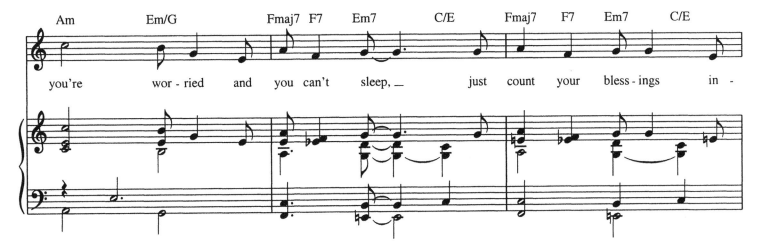

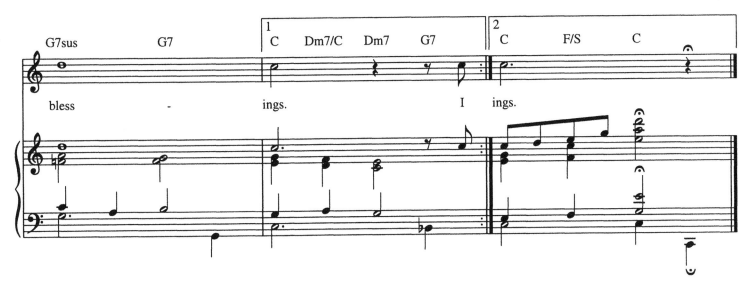

Choreography

Words and Music by
IRVING BERLIN

Moderately

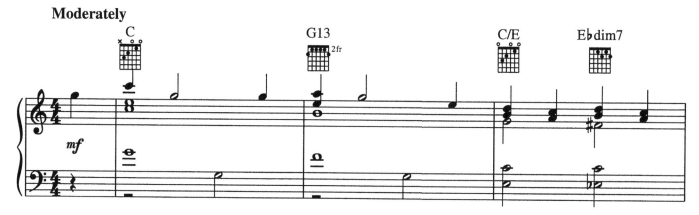

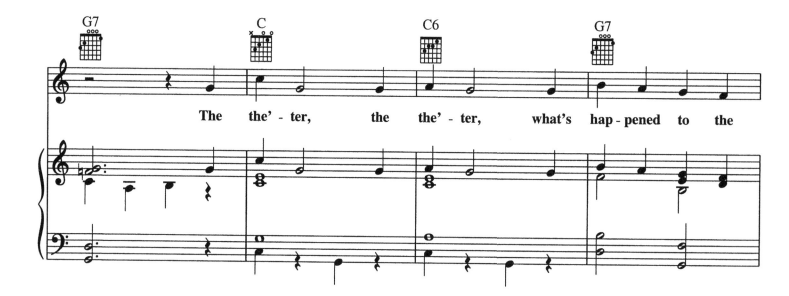

The the'-ter, the the'-ter, what's hap-pened to the

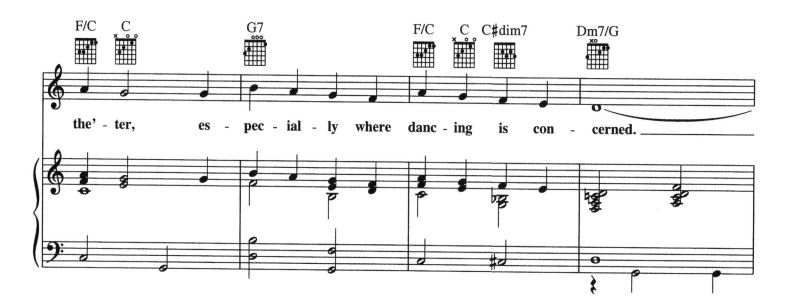

the'-ter, es-pec-ial-ly where danc-ing is con-cerned.

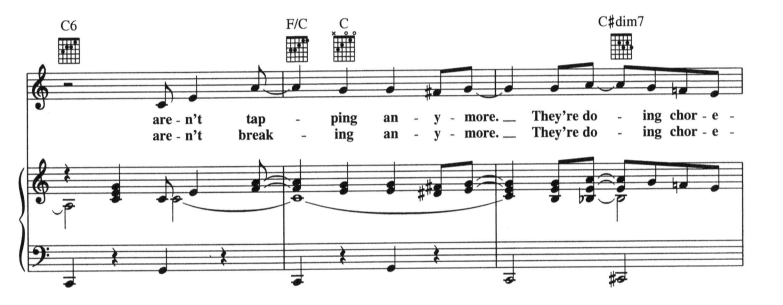

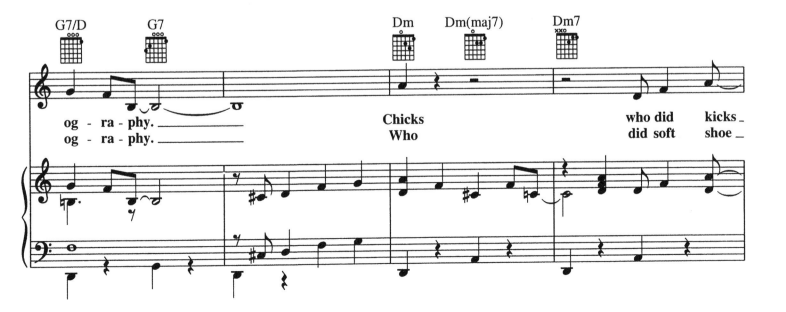

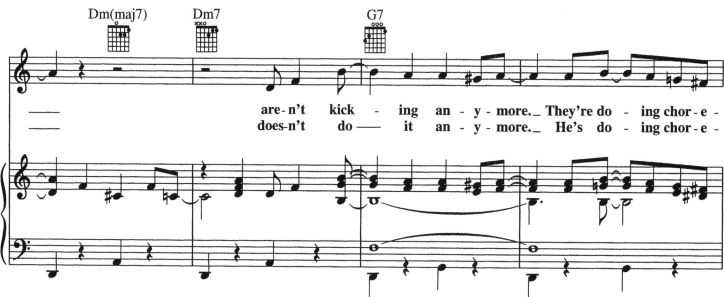

are-n't kick - ing an - y - more._ They're do - ing chor - e -
does-n't do _ it an - y - more._ He's do - ing chor - e -

og - ra - phy. _____ Queens with rou - tines_
og - ra - phy. _____ Heps who did steps_

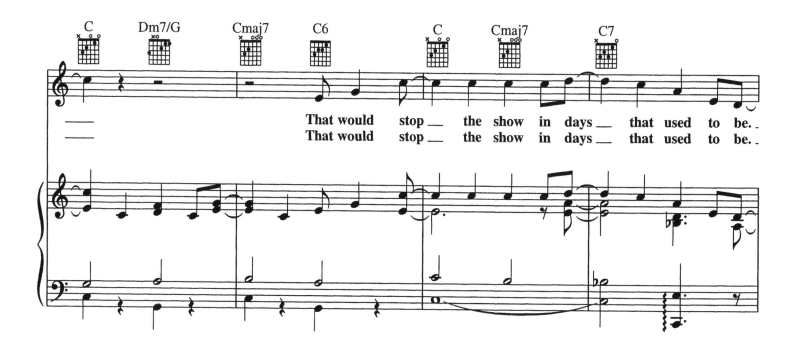

That would stop _ the show in days _ that used to be._
That would stop _ the show in days _ that used to be._

One and all ___ they're not chanc - ing ___
Through the air ___ they keep fly - ing —

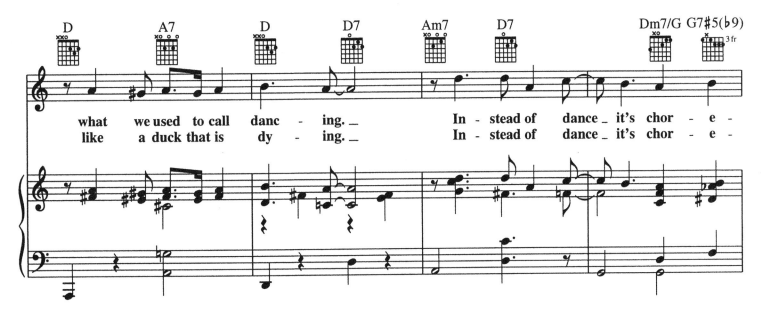

what we used to call danc - ing. ___ In - stead of dance _ it's chor - e -
like a duck that is dy - ing. ___ In - stead of dance _ it's chor - e -

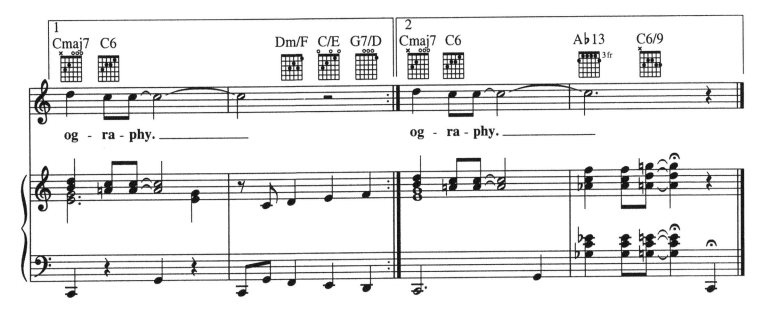

og - ra - phy. _____

og - ra - phy. _____

Gee, I Wish I Was Back in the Army

Words and Music by
IRVING BERLIN

Heat Wave

Words and Music by
IRVING BERLIN

Love, You Didn't Do Right by Me

Words and Music by
IRVING BERLIN

The Old Man

Words and Music by
IRVING BERLIN

Slowly and gangy

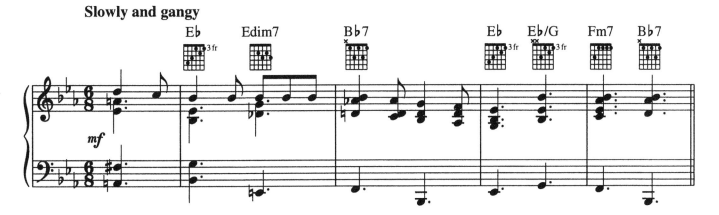

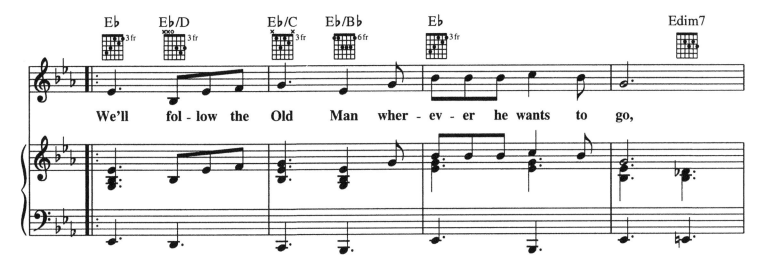

We'll fol-low the Old Man wher-ev-er he wants to go,

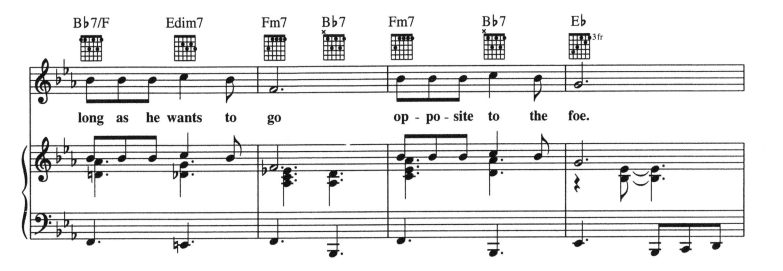

long as he wants to go op-po-site to the foe.

Mandy

Words and Music by
IRVING BERLIN

40

Sisters

Words and Music by
IRVING BERLIN

White Christmas

Words and Music by
IRVING BERLIN

The sun is shin - ing, the grass is green, _ the

or - ange and palm trees sway. There's nev - er been such a

day in Bev - er - ly Hills, L. A.

Snow

Words and Music by
IRVING BERLIN

54

White Christmas

Produced by Robert Emmett Dolan
Directed by Michael Curtiz
Music & Lyrics by Irving Berlin
Choreography by Robert Alton
Cinematography by Loyal Griggs (Technicolor, VistaVision)
Released by Paramount Pictures, August 1954
Color, 120 minutes

Cast

Bing Crosby	*Bob Wallace*
Danny Kaye	*Phil Davis*
Rosemary Clooney	*Betty Haynes*
Vera-Ellen	*Judy Haynes*
Dean Jagger	*General Waverly*
Mary Wickes	*Emma*
John Brascia	*Joe*
Anne Whitfield	*Susan*